EPOXY RESIN ART FOR BEGINNERS

A step-by-step Guide to Working with Resin Including DIY Masterpiece to Realize at Home | How to Create Epoxy Sculptures and Crafts such as Jewelry, Tabletops, Paintings, and Much More!

Lily Woodhall

Epoxy Resin Art for Beginners

© 2023 by **Lily Woodhall**

ALL RIGHTS RESERVED

No part of this book may be reproduced, distributed, or transmitted in any form or by any means without the prior written permission of the publisher, except in the case of brief quotations embodied in critical reviews and certain other noncommercial uses permitted by copyright law.

TABLE OF CONTENTS

About the Author 4
Introduction 5
What is Epoxy Resin Art? 7
Essential Resin Art Tools for Beginners 9
Choosing the Right Resin 30
Safety Precautions 35
Basic Techniques and Fundamentals 40
Building Epoxy Casting Mold and Proper Curing Methods for Epoxy 56
DIY Resin Art Projects for Beginners 62
Advanced Projects 88
Troubleshooting and Tips 112
Epoxy Resin Brand and Suppliers 116
Conclusion 121

ABOUT THE AUTHOR

Lily Woodhall is a passionate artist and creative enthusiast who has dedicated her artistic journey to the captivating world of epoxy resin art. With years of experience in mastering resin techniques, Lily brings a wealth of knowledge and hands-on expertise to this book.

Her love for crafting, combined with her dedication to sharing her skills, makes her the perfect guide for beginners eager to explore the limitless possibilities of epoxy resin. Lily's step-by-step approach and commitment to nurturing artistic talent make her a trusted mentor in the world of resin art.

Through this book, she invites readers to embark on their artistic adventures, unlocking their creative potential one resin project at a time.

INTRODUCTION

Have you ever wondered how to create something truly mesmerizing, a work of art that captures your imagination and reflects your unique vision? There's a secret waiting to be unveiled. And it's hidden within the pages of this book. Within these pages lies the key to a world where liquid transforms into magic—a world where everyday objects become the canvas for your imagination, a world where the ordinary becomes extraordinary.

Epoxy resin, a captivating material, is at the heart of this journey. It's the medium that allows you to breathe life into your creative dreams, even if you've never considered yourself an artist. It's a substance that defies expectations, turning simplicity into sophistication and bringing your ideas to life in ways you've never imagined.

But this book isn't just about what epoxy resin is or how it works. It's about what it can do for you, and the endless possibilities it offers to turn your artistic aspirations into reality. If you're searching for a new creative outlet, a way to add a personal touch to your gifts, or simply an exciting adventure, you've found it right here.

I will be your guide and your artistic mentor through this journey. With years of experience and a passion for resin artistry, I'm here to lead you through a world of wonder and imagination. Together, we'll embark on a journey that begins with simple curiosity and leads to your discovery of creative superpowers.

In the coming chapters, you'll find secrets and surprises, challenges and inspirations. You'll be equipped with the knowledge, tools, and techniques to turn resin into enchantment. You'll unveil the potential hidden within your hands as you mold, shape, and transform epoxy resin into works of art.

But the real magic lies ahead, beyond these introductory words. Each chapter holds a piece of the puzzle, and as you turn the pages, you'll uncover the mysteries of epoxy resin art one after the other. It's a journey that promises not just artistic satisfaction but also a sense of accomplishment as you create unique, breathtaking pieces that are uniquely yours.

So, are you ready to embark on this artistic adventure, to awaken the artist within you, and explore the boundless world of epoxy resin artistry? The magic of this journey awaits, and the secrets within these pages are yours to uncover. Let's dive in and unveil the wonders of "Epoxy Resin Art for Beginners" together.

I wish you all the best in your pursuit!

CHAPTER

1

WHAT IS EPOXY RESIN ART?

Resin art is the new painting style that doesn't require using a brush, painting board, or known painting materials to create an artwork. Epoxy Resin Art combines the runny chemical known as epoxy resin with different color pigments and additives to create unique patterns and textures.

When making the resin, you will have to mix it with hardener, making it harden gradually over time and become a solid plastic. Resin is durable; the final product you will produce after all the procedures will give you a high gloss protective medium that you can use for various purposes. Epoxy resin is normally used in art to seal a variety of works, including drawings, photographs, and oil paintings, to create a beautiful ultra-protective varnish.

What will surprise you is that epoxy resin has a great history that dates back to many decades ago. The resin of nature, also known as amber, is produced using trees and fossilizes to develop a hard and transparent slab. And amber has been considered a decorative item since the beginning of time many centuries ago. Today, many more modern versions of resins are being created every day.

Epoxy resin was first discovered in the 1930s when people realized they could use this art to adhere items together or preserve an object. Later, resin made a name in the art world and became among the sought-after art pieces among older and younger generations. So you may be wondering what resin is made of. Well, the resin is a viscous liquid produced when trees produce oil due to injury.

These oils, when exposed to air, become oxidized and form a thick, sticky fluid known as resin. The history of resin has never stopped there. In Greece, it was commonly used as a primitive form of chewing gum to get a fresh breath. Resin art uses epoxy resin, which can be improvised as natural resin. Epoxy Resin has a two-part system of synthetic polymer resin and a hardener. After you combine these two chemicals, they will experience a chemical reaction that hardens them to form a solid art.

CHAPTER 2

ESSENTIAL RESIN ART TOOLS FOR BEGINNERS

As a beginner, you may find it overwhelming to think of where to start, especially since many resin tools are available. Each resin tool has a purpose, and many are out there. You must do a good job whenever you are trying to make a piece to save money, effort, and time, and this can only be achieved through appropriate tools.

Also, you have to bear in mind that just because you are a beginner doesn't mean you must struggle to find the right tools for your projects. You may look for some of these tools online or in stores. But amazingly, you even have some out of your home without knowing. In this chapter, we will talk about the necessary tools you need to create a resin art project.

The first step in getting resin tools is to look for plastic ones. Plastic resin-based tools offer many significant benefits, including resin doesn't stick to plastic, which makes it easy to clean. You can also use the plastic tools as often as you want. When you finish using the tools, there are two cleaning options you can use.

Spray isopropyl alcohol on the tools to wet them, then use a dry paper towel to wipe them. Once they are free from resins, use hot, soapy water to wash them and let them dry completely before you use them again, or lay wet tools on the used plastic tool and allow the resin to cure overnight. You can use any of these options depending on which you find easy.

So, with much being said, let's look at the essential resin tool you can use when crafting your project.

Respirator mask

Although it's not all resin that is toxic, you still need to wear a respirator mask when you are dealing with epoxy resin. Inhaling resin vapor for a long time can irritate your respiratory tract. You may start feeling itching and seedling, so you must be cautious when using it regularly. If highly concentrated resin touches your eyelids or skin, it can cause itching and swelling.

But it's only a small population that got affected by resin allergies. It's similar to a peanut allergy. People allergic to it can experience varying discomfort; some feel itching while others might feel swelling. To be on the safe side, use a respiratory mask that is approved by the National Institute for Occupational Safety and Health (NIOSH) whenever you are going to work with epoxy resin and one that fits you properly.

OLD CLOTHES OR APRON

As I said, some things you need for your resin project can be found at home. You can use old clothes or an apron made from rubber for extra protection. When resin touches your clothes, it's challenging to get rid of them, so it's better to wear something that you know even if it gets spoiled, it won't bother you. Also, you should wear clothes with long sleeves to prevent the resin from touching your body. If you have long hair, tie it into a ponytail so the resin won't touch your hair.

DISPOSABLE GLOVES

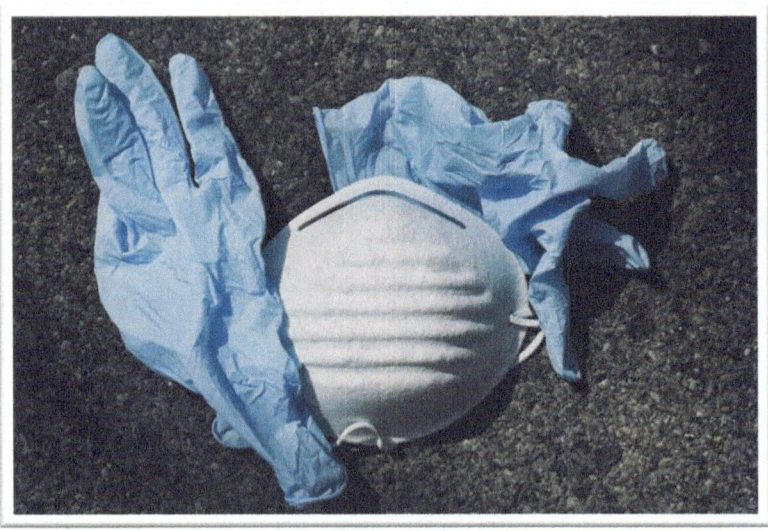

Disposable gloves can go a great way in protecting your hand from getting resin, which can cause itching and skin irritation. Also, resin is sticky naturally, so when you put a pair of gloves in your hand, keep some beside you in case the ones you wear are messed up. If you get small resins on your hand, wash it off immediately. If you want strong gloves, you can consider nitrile gloves. Their durability and nature are similar to latex gloves. However, they offer more protection because they are stronger than latex gloves and don't contain allergens like latex gloves. If you have sensitive skin, you can use barrier lotion on your body before you wear the gloves.

SAFETY GOGGLE

Your eyes are valuable assets, so you must protect them at all costs. Safety goggles are the best protective mechanism you can use. They will protect your eyes from fumes and toxins. Amazingly, safety glasses are inexpensive. Therefore, you can get one or two or even plenty to keep in case one gets spoiled.

MASKING TAPE

Masking tape usually helps catch drips. You can use a good quality painter's tape to tape the bottom of your work, especially if you resin the sides. Normally, drips will build around the bottom and edge of your project. To make a good finish, you can use masking tape for the areas. Once the resin dries, you can remove the tape.

PLASTIC DROP SHEET

You can find plastic drop sheets in a hardware store. Check the painting aisle. This sheet can protect your floor and working surface from spills that may stick permanently. If a plastic drop sheet is inexpensive, you can look for a smooth, clear vinyl shower curtain as an alternative. The curtain can be used more than once, which offers more benefits than the drop sheet. Other alternatives besides vinyl shower curtains include a garbage bag cut and spread open, a drawer liner, a silicone mat, and kitchen parchment paper for smaller projects. You can use isopropyl alcohol to clean resin when it spills on your floor or working surface. If they dry out, you can leave it and clean the next day.

PLASTIC MEASURING CUP

A plastic measuring cup can be used to measure your resin mixtures. This will give you an accurate measurement of the ingredients you will use for your project. Resin and hardener will never mix properly if you don't measure them accurately. So, use a measuring cup to avoid making mistakes when measuring. You can also measure any ingredients first. Whether you measure the resin or the hardener first, it won't make any difference. The goal is to measure them equally. Once you finish mixing, turn the measuring cup upside down to let the resin pool. This will enable the resin to set before the following day. When the next day approaches, you can peel it off easily, and your measuring cup will be ready for reuse.

PLASTIC SPREADER

Even though resin will naturally self-level after pouring it, you can still use a plastic spreader to distribute it evenly over your project. You can use an old paintbrush to apply the resin to small areas or a toothpick or popsicle sticks. If you also wish to set the resin in a dome and prevent it from spilling over the sides. Use a small spatula to move the resin to the edges or a small knife. You can also use your gloved hand to put the resins on the sides of your artwork.

PLASTIC CONTAINER FOR WATER

If your resin is colder than room temperature, it's not advisable to use it. Instead, use a plastic container to warm it. To prevent the bottles from tipping over, use a narrow container that has high edges. Fill the container halfway with warm water, then insert the capped bottles and leave it to get warm for 10-15 minutes. Beware of letting your resin come in contact with water because if that happens, it won't cure. Before you open the bottles, start measuring and mixing after thoroughly drying the bottles.

DUST COVER

Before making your resin, it's best to have a dust cover nearby. This will prevent your freshly done work from getting exposed, especially when you must step out for a moment amidst the work. Clean the cover to eliminate any dust that can fall into your work. You can use cardboard boxes or plastic containers. But carbon boxes are riskier because they can easily flop drops on top of the resin, and plastic containers are easier to clean. So, if you must use the cardboard box, remove the flaps before you begin.

BUTANE TORCH

One of the problems that people often encounter while working with resin is air bubbles. These bubbles can appear at any stage of your work, and you must eliminate them to prevent them from curing and becoming part of your work. To achieve this, get a butane torch. You can also use a straw or toothpick to blow them or poke them, but it's time-consuming and not as effective as using the butane torch. Alternatively, you can use a hair dryer, but it's also not as effective as butane touch because when using a hair dryer, there are chances that it can blow dust into your work and ruin the glass-like finish you will get later. A heat gun is another great solution when you are dealing with silicone molds for resin that contains alcohol ink. It will give you the desired heat, but it still poses a risk of stirring particles into your work. So the best here is the butane or flame touch, and you can get it from any nearby hardware store.

PLASTIC STIR/MIXING STICK

Plastic sticks will help you mix your resin and prevent it from getting sticky. Using under-mix resin will not cure properly. Scrape the side of the container to ensure every ingredient is mixed and well combined. Using a plastic stir or a mixing stick will do this job for you better than a round object.

HAND CLEANER

If resin touches your skin, clean it as quickly as possible. Resin can stick to your hand, but you can eliminate it with a hand cleaner, which you can purchase from any store nearby. You can also dry rub your hand to remove the resin using salt or poppyseeds and liquid soap, then use water to rinse it.

PAPER TOWELS AND ALCOHOL

You can clean spills and clean up with paper towels and isopropyl alcohol. Alcohol will break the resin residue, which can make it easy to be wiped clean. Soak a paper towel inside alcohol while covering your hands with gloves. Never dip your free hand inside an alcohol to clean resin. Alcohol can easily be absorbed into your skin and cause damage. You should also never let resin go down the sink.

TOOTHPICK

A toothpick is another must-have tool for resining. Once you are done with your art and make all the necessary touches, inspect and watch it closely. The toothpick will help you pop bubbles or remove dust specks. A toothpick can also assist you in pushing small resins around or inserting inclusions like dry flowers or gemstones perfectly.

ALCOHOL INK

Alcohol ink is used when you want to add beautiful coloration to your resin. There are many ways you can achieve the desired coloration using alcohol. You can add it directly to the mixture, add it to your working surface, then spread the resin on top of it, or come up with your own unique way of using it. Keep in mind that alcohol can fade over time with resin. Therefore, if you wish to preserve it, use a UV protectant.

ACRYLIC PAINT

If you wish to add color to your resin, you can use acrylic paint. But ensure you don't use more than 10% colorant to the resin. Adding more than necessary will chemically alter the resin mixtures. And be careful while mixing to avoid forming bubbles.

PAINT PEN

You can use a paint pen to add embellishments or details to your project. Particularly, they are used when drawing agate and geode lines in resin geode creation. Many paint pens are available in the market, so you have to be careful when purchasing one. Ensure you buy from a reputable brand to use it for a long time.

Glitter

If you want to add shine to your work. You can use glitters. Like paint pens, purchase glitters from a well-known brand—one with various holographic colors, which can give you a glow even in darker shades.

SILICON RESIN MOLDS

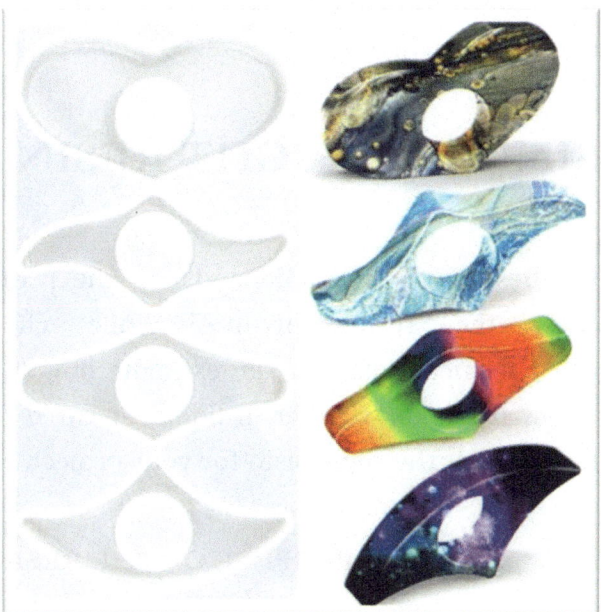

Resin is a perfect material for creating all sorts of crafts. But it can be tricky at the same time. Among the most important tools you need is a silicon resin mold. Its flexibility enables it to be an easy material to use for popping resin pieces. Silicon molds are also not sticky. You don't have to worry about your resin sticking to the mold, and silicon molds usually come in various shapes and sizes. Use them to unleash your creativity when using them.

CHAPTER
3

CHOOSING THE RIGHT RESIN

Finding the best epoxy resin depends on the properties that characterize the resin mixture. While checking the manufacturer's specifications, you can estimate how the resin can be used and how it works, whether in liquid or cured form. Below are ways you can select the right resin for your project.

THE INTENDED PURPOSE OF THE RESIN

The first step in choosing an epoxy resin is to outline the physical requirements like environmental conditions, potential stressors, chemical exposures, and expected product service life. How strong do you need the part to be, does it need to be flexible, and do you wish the product to withstand the usual pleasure level or weight? Will you expose the product to extreme conditions, and what's its life expectancy?

ARE THERE SPECIAL AESTHETIC CONSIDERATIONS?

Choosing the best material for your work includes selecting material that will exhibit color, transparency, texture, and the kind of surface you want to have. When choosing epoxy resin, check and ensure it will meet your requirements. Does it have the transparency and color you need? Does it have the texture or finish you need? Do you have an existing color that can match many more?

DO ANY REGULATORY REQUIREMENTS APPLY?

An important aspect of selecting resin is to check the regulatory requirements and applications. For instance, if you will transport the resin internationally or incorporate it into a high-performance engineering application. Ensure that the materials you choose meet the industry requirements. What kind of regulations does it need to meet? Is it FDA, RoHS, NSF, or REACH? Do you need to make the product safe for children, or must it be food-safe?

LOW-VISCOSITY EPOXY RESIN

The word viscosity means the flowability of liquid. However, you need to be careful when using this. Generally, you say a liquid has low viscosity when it's thin and flowing freely. When buying a low-viscosity resin, select a low-viscosity epoxy resin. For certain applicants, they must use an almost watery consistency, which is important. For instance, when you want to cast molds or make river tables. Low-viscosity epoxy resin usually cures slowly, therefore;

you must plan your time. Moreover, you have more time for the processing. This will stop you from getting stressed.

Additionally, since the exothermic chemical transformation process is slow, it releases little heat. This is different from the high-viscosity resin. Using the low viscosity, you can create a thicker layer and a larger amount at a step.

The best areas to use a low-casting epoxy resin include casting molds, manufacturing epoxy resin jewelry, and creating molded parts when making models. It's also used when producing epoxy resin tables and resin river tables, filling cracks and holes in wood with epoxy, and producing epoxy resin floors for living areas or garage floors.

Viscous epoxy resins

The consistency of highly viscous epoxy resin is similar to honey. When you go to the market to purchase a viscous epoxy resin, the sellers don't refer to it as highly viscous but as laminating resin or just resin. They are suitable for coating surfaces. Still, you can also use them to realize projects in resin art fields and geodes.

When using highly viscous epoxy resins, follow the manufacturer's instructions about the maximum layer you must use during each step. In many situations and for trouble-free processing, you only need one or two maximum layers of thickness. The various arts you can use high-viscosity resin include the casting of paintings with epoxy resin, deco items like resin geode and resin Petri dishes, finishing of paintings and works of art of different sorts: some epoxy resin jewelry, sealing surfaces like worktops or tables.

THE DIFFERENT VISCOSITY OF EPOXY RESIN

Thickness layer

You can easily cast thicker layers, particularly with low-viscosity epoxy resins, because the low viscosity doesn't heat much while curing. If the resin forms bubbles, you can easily use some of the tools we mentioned for air bubbles to eliminate them. Also, you should not pour high-viscosity resin thicker than one centimeter because if it forms bubbles, it will be hard for you to make them rise and escape from the resin.

Processing time

Processing time, also known as pot time or open time, is another important factor to consider when choosing the right resin for your project. The processing time indicates the time frame within which the resin will be processed after you mix it with the hardener. You should not use thick and tough resin except on special occasions. Because if you do, it will not color homogeneously and won't be distributed evenly on a flat surface.

Pros of short processing time include the fact that you can reach certain effects when using this resin, and it also creates a fast layer since you can pour several layers on top of one another quickly. The disadvantages of using this resin are that it has difficult venting solutions, which lead to more bubbles, and it doesn't form yellow coloration under UV- irradiation.

On the other hand, the benefits of using a long processing time resin include having adequate them to mix many resins and also working on them quietly and peacefully. When you decide to layer on top layers, the transition will be less visible. The only disadvantage of the long processing time resin is that you will need more materials to cast many layers.

Curing time

After mixing the components, the time it takes to reach a stage of hardness and insensitivity is the curing time. In most cases, there is a correlation between the curing time and the processing time. If the processing time is short, the resin will cure completely no matter how short the time is.

CHAPTER 4

SAFETY PRECAUTIONS

Resin is a good material to create many crafts, but while using it, you must be cautious. Here are some safety precautions you should note when using resin mixture.

WEAR GLOVES

Glove is one of the important tools you should always have when you want to start a project. The gloves will protect your hand from epoxy resin and hardener liquids. When the resin and hardener come in contact with your skin, they can cause swelling, itching, or skin irritation.

You can use nitrile gloves or latex gloves. If you carefully remove the gloves after using them, you can clean them and later reuse them. If, unfortunately, you get resin on your hand, you can use baby wipes to clean it. After that, then use soap and water to clean the remaining residues. You can use a pumice soap when the resin becomes too sticky.

HAVE GOOD VENTILATION IN YOUR AREA

While thinking about the benefits of ventilation for resin, you should think of it as a lab animal. You need ventilation. This also applies to resin. It's good to be in a space with good ventilation. Create one or two windows in your workplace so air will move in and out of the room. Turn on your fan whenever you are working, especially if you can't open windows. Alternatively, you can use a desk fan or any fan to ensure air movement in the room.

Wear plastic apron

Another important safety tool you need is a plastic apron. When you are working with resin, spills, and drips can happen. It's awful to ruin your favorite clothes, and the unfortunate part is that you won't even know when it happens until you want to wash the clothes, or after washing, you will realize it has a spill or resin on it. The best resin apron you should purchase is made from PVC. Even if resin spills on it, you can peel or clean it off immediately.

Wear safety goggles

Safety glasses are among the inexpensive ways you can protect yourself from harmful chemicals that are in resin. You can buy these glasses from any shop that sells accessories near you.

Use respiratory mask

Although many resins don't require you to use a respiratory mask, remember that these are chemicals we are talking about. Even if it's not harmful to others, it might affect your skin and respiratory tract, especially if you have a weak immune system. Additionally, some of these resins are odorless, but just because you can't smell them doesn't mean they aren't harmful. Protect your respiratory system by using a respirator mask. But before you buy any mask, ensure it is a NIOSH-approved respirator for fumes. You can buy a small mask as a beginner since you won't come into contact with the chemicals often.

Use resin for arts and crafts

When you buy resin, ensure it has 'conform to ASTM D-4236' designation on its label. This indicates that it's for arts and crafts usage. You should not purchase any product that doesn't have this mark. Avoid those companies that lead you to believe that you can put this thing on as a moisturizer because they are mostly the same people who will not have the design.

Have access to the resin kit's safety data sheets

When you start your craft creation journey using resin, one of the important things you should get your hands on is the resin kit's safety data sheet. The sheet usually contains information on the people you can contact in emergencies. Never use a resin whose company has not shared their safety data sheets because it shows they are hiding something.

Never ingest epoxy

After you finish using epoxy resin, thoroughly wash your hands before you eat or drink anything using your hands. If by mistake you swallow epoxy, consume a large quantity of water and never induce vomiting. Hardeners are corrosive. So, they can cause further harm if you try to vomit them. Contact a professional healthcare provider or Poison Control center.

Work clean

Always maintain a clean working environment to avoid getting in contact with resin accidentally. If you have resin residue on your gloves, avoid touching doors, handles, light switches, or other containers because you may probably touch them again when not wearing gloves. It can lead to disaster if you accidentally consume it.

When the residue spills, clean it as fast as possible and ensure you don't leave any remnant on the surface it spills, then follow up with a paper towel. Avoid using sawdust or other fine cellulose materials to absorb hardener. Instead, use sand, clay, or any inert absorbent material. Clean resin or mix it with lacquer thinner, acetone, or alcohol. Check the solvent container and follow the precautions they wrote there. Use warm, soapy water to clean hardener residue.

SAFETY PRECAUTIONS WHEN DISPOSING OF EPOXY RESIN

When you are done using resin, and there is remaining, puncture the corner of it and drain it into a new container. Avoid disposing of resin or hardeners in their liquid form. Mix them and let them cure to an inert solid before you dispose of them.

A curing epoxy pot can get hot enough to start emitting hazardous fumes. This can easily ignite combustible materials if there are any nearby. You should put epoxy pots in a well-ventilated room away from your working space and combustible materials.

EPOXY-RELATED HAZARD

Uncontrolled curing of epoxy

When you cure epoxy with an exothermic chemical, it can emit heat. If you leave it to cure in a contained mass like a mixing pot, this epoxy can get hot and melt plastic, burn you, or ignite combustible materials. The larger or thicker the epoxy mass, the hotter it can generate.

For example, a 200g mixed epoxy mass can generate up to 800J heat. As mixed resin and hardener thermally decompose, they get hotter and frothier, generating harmful substances like carbon monoxide, oxides of nitrogen, ammonia, and even aldehydes sometimes. Only use a flame with resins when it's your last resort, and work in a well-ventilated space.

When the leftover is curing, please keep it where you will monitor it. Use a fan to disperse the vapor and direct them from where people frequent. Air-purifying respirators might not be enough for this job. You need a highly ventilated space. Avoid combining hardener with sawdust or wood chips, which can lead to fire. Because both the air and moisture will react with an amine. Avoid pouring the mixture on a dustbin that has sawdust inside.

Spraying epoxy

It's not safe to spray epoxy. You must be cautious when using a spray gun because epoxy leaves a spray gun nozzle and becomes a small fine mist that can be easily inhaled into the respiratory system. This can lead to severe lung damage and other health issues. The mist can settle on your skin and cause irritation, itching, or swelling. It can also enter your eyes and lead to problems. Normally, spraying epoxy elevates the amount of unwanted substances released compared to other methods. Using solvent to thin the epoxy can increase the health and safety risk. If you must spray resins, use an air-supplied ventilator and wear full body protection clothes.

CHAPTER

5

BASIC TECHNIQUES AND FUNDAMENTALS

As a beginner in epoxy resin art, you need to familiarize yourself with its fundamentals and basic techniques. Knowing this could make your journey smoother and faster. In fact, it will make you more efficient and creative. Do you even know that epoxy resin can be used in many ways? You can use it as a filler, sealer, and adhesive to mold and create many beautiful projects.

However, you must be able to answer a big question as a beginner. The question is, how you can successfully and effectively use resin without making errors? Rest assured, in this chapter, we will explore the basic techniques and fundamentals for using epoxy resin.

Let's dive into the details.

GETTING READY TO USE EPOXY RESIN

In the previous chapters, I shared the necessary tools you need for precautions before you start using resin. Now, grab your protective equipment, wear them, and ensure you work in a well-ventilated space. Once you are done with these safety precautions, set up your working space and arrange the materials you need to use.

Keep your rollers and brushes nearby so you won't have to go to and fro to get them after you start the work. Mix the epoxy using a spatula or paint stirrer. Mix it in a bucket if you spread it on a large surface. Clean the surface you wish to pour the resin before you pour it to eliminate dirt or dust that can affect your final product.

Ensure the surface is dry before you apply the resin. Remember, when mixing the epoxy resin, follow the instructions and guidelines written on the kit and ensure it is thoroughly mixed before you use it. Keep in mind that you must get rid of any resin that touches your skin immediately.

Using resin to seal a surface

You can use epoxy resin for different purposes. For instance, if you have a metal that has started rusting, you can use resin to seal it or if you wish to add a durable layer on your surface or floor. Resin can be a great tool to use and achieve the desired look you want in your space. Also, if you want to add some beautiful touches, things like paint, mica, and glitter can be a great addition.

For a concrete floor, you must use a specific resin, which is thin and low-viscosity resin. To apply the resin to the floor, use smooth and broad strokes. This will increase the durability of your concrete, making it last longer than its initial lifespan. If, while using the resin, bubbles form, use a toothpick to pop it to make your work smoother.

Additionally, you can use resin seals to protect your tables and wooden doors. For bigger doors, use foam rollers. For tables, you can use a paintbrush to put the epoxy resin coating. After the resin cures, it will protect the doors and tables and to make them shine.

The resin will also follow the stained wood color to enhance its durability.

If there is a crack in the surface, use a toothpick, which ideally is supposed to be part of the equipment you prepared for your work. Once the resin cures, the crack will be sealed completely and waterproof. The incredible aspect of resin didn't stop there. If you have epoxy flooring, then it can also be used to create decorative patterns. All you need to do is put a colored stone or vinyl chip in a pattern and use a resin mixture to cover it.

Because the resin is clear, it will enable people to see and appreciate the colored stone or chip through the protective and glossy layer if you are worried about slipping because applying resin to any surface will make it non-slip, even if it was slippery before. This means if in your home you have a slippery surface, you can use resin to cover it and protect yourself and your family from tripping or falling.

After you finish everything, let the resin dry overnight. However, resin brands will have different drying times, but most need several hours to dry. So, whichever you purchase, let it dry for at least 8 hours. You can also check the package for the specific time it requires to dry. If you wish to make it dry quickly on a fan, point it towards the work.

How to use resin as an adhesive

Resin is an excellent bonding agent that you can apply. Additionally, epoxy resin is an amazing versatile adhesive and bonding agent that can help you retain your item's bonding, and make it stronger. It can be used to repair and connect parts. Also, there is another important thing you should take note of. After mixing epoxy resin, you should use it immediately because if you leave it too long, it will chemically react and become hard, making it difficult to use. As I said, the time it usually takes to harden depends on the product and manufacturer.

Fix loose-fitting joints in furniture using epoxy resin. You can use epoxy to fix joints in furniture without losing its strength. Brush the epoxy resin layer onto the parts you wish to join, then assemble the furniture back and let the resin cure. For instance, if you have a loose-fitting chair and you wish to join it, use resin and then assemble the parts. When applying, use a brush and ensure the epoxy resin is specifically made for furniture.

The versatility of epoxy resin doesn't stop there because you can use it to repair even small items like cups, aside from creating unique masterpieces. For example, if you have a cup whose hand is broken, you can apply the resin on the broken parts. Then, you can join them together and allow it to dry. This will make the cup more durable and usable.

Furthermore, if you have a fiberglass that needs repair, epoxy resin can do that trick for you. The small fiber in fiberglass perfectly bonds with resin. So, if you have any fiberglass items you wish to repair, use resin to do that. Apply it and let it cure, and you have successfully retrieved your item back to its original shape. If you use epoxy in an item that is exposed to sunlight, like an airplane, put the resin on the inner side of the fiberglass, which is not exposed to sunlight because ultraviolet rays from sunlight can reduce the durability of the resin.

You can also use resin to connect jewelry pieces. If you have broken jewelry and you don't wish to throw it away, epoxy resin can be your life saver by helping you repair the piece and use it again. For instance, if a pearl gets separated from your earrings, you can reattach it again using a resin mixture. You can also use epoxy resin to design a brand new jewelry.

Lastly, the juicy part is making art with resin. Mix resin and pour it into a mold with a flower or insect inside. You can use anything of your choice aside from flowers and insects. For the mold, you can use items like ice cubes, insert the flower or decorative thing inside, pour the resin, and fill the mold.

Once it cures, remove it and display it in your place of choice. For example, if you are an insect lover and want to create an insect art. You can look for insects like beetles and then put them in the mold.

Fill the mold with an epoxy mixture and create a unique insect art. Since resin is durable, your art will last longer than you can imagine.

Place a picture in a mold to create an epoxy picture. Another aspect of using epoxy resin is that you can preserve a precious memory you want. Do you have a picture you don't want anything to happen to? And do you know putting it inside an album is no longer an option? Resin will be of great benefit to achieve this. Just get a mold inside the picture and then pour the resin mixture. It will create a square mold, allowing it to stand independently after you display it.

Cover a painted canvas with epoxy to create a textured painting. Just brush a layer of epoxy resin on the painting. If you want more texture in some areas, add a thick resin layer.

Tips on Mixing and Pouring Resin

Your procedure for mixing epoxy is the biggest factor determining your success or failure. Any slight mistake can alter your final result. So, you must be careful when mixing epoxy. Below are some tips for mixing epoxy resin.

The correct mixing ratio

First, note that epoxy usually has a mixing ratio depending on the manufacturers. You will always find the mixing ratio written on the resin package. Sometimes, you will find the mixing ratio to be 1:1 or 2:1. Sometimes, the manufacturer's specifications might be slightly complicated with mixing ratio variations like 100-45. For this, you should always make sure you read the manufacturer's instructions before you mix the ingredients.

Mix by volume instead of weight

Depending on the brand you purchase, chances are the resin and hardener differ in density. This means they don't have the same weight. If the two ingredients have different weights and the mixing ratio is 1:1, it means there might be a mistake somewhere since they have different weights.

Observe ambient temperature

Casting resin is a heat-sensitive element. So, you must be careful of the ambient temperature when mixing the ingredients. For example, an ambient temperature below 20° means the resin will cure slowly, and a waxy layer can form on the surface. You must remove it first before you process the resin, and removing it is not an easy task.

If the temperature drops further than 20°, the resin will probably crystallize. At a temperature above 20°, the resin reaction time will significantly increase. This time doesn't only apply to the curing time, but the material will be processed further. So, it's best to go for a product with a longer processing time.

If your workplace is outdoors and you have the epoxy outside to stay overnight, the curing time will be longer, especially if the temperature drops at night. The dew also caused by temperature differences can influence the resin negatively and the quality of the surface material.

Observe humidity

Just as the temperature can affect resin, humidity also affects the resin mixture. For example, if the humidity is above 65%, ensure you put the mixture inside an airtight container to prevent it from coming in contact with air. If not, use the material immediately. This effect can also affect the mixture if it's opened and constantly closed because each time you open it, oxygen will enter the container and react with the hardener. Also, this means you should handle resin and hardeners with clean tools if you apply them on a moisture surface like concrete and prime the substrate in advance.

To ensure your resin is optimally processed, store it for about 12 hours at a temperature of 20° to 25° maximum. If you can't achieve this storage period, you can bring it to the correct temperature using the water bath method. This step is important if you want to get a satisfactory result because using cold resin will lead to the formation of air bubbles, which can greatly affect your end product.

Be careful when mixing the components

Mixing of resin is an essential factor in determining your final result. So, you must be careful. Note that a lot of resin sticks to the edge of the mixing container. Therefore, you should always mix a high amount of resin and use a mixing stick to get all the ones that stick to the edges.

Choose the right tools when mixing

The best tool to use when mixing epoxy should have straight sides. This will allow it to mix thoroughly even if the ingredients stick to the edges of the container. If you are mixing small quantities, a flat spatula will be the best choice. For small mixing or as a beginner, you can always use a cheap wooden spatula. As you advance, you can purchase a special epoxy mixing tool with the advantage of reusing it. The special mixing tools are also designed to prevent air from entering the mixture, but you should only buy or use the tool when mixing large or medium quantities of resin.

Only use high-quality Epoxy Resins

Whether you are a beginner or an advanced user, always use a high-quality resin. No matter how tempted you are to buy low-quality products, try to buy the big ones to have a good result, even as a beginner. If you buy cheap projects, you will regret it later because they often have yellowish coloration and do not cure or process properly. Therefore, you should always stick to this principle: Buy big and have a good result.

Use only compatible Resins

Using resin and hardeners from the same manufacturers will give you a satisfactory result because they are meant for each other. One mistake you should never make unless there is no way out is mixing resin and hardener from different brands because it can lead to unexpected chemical reactions, which can be disastrous.

Use only compatible Colorants

Not all colorants are compatible with particular resins. So, when coloring the resin, ensure you use a compatible colorant to avoid having undesirable results.

Observe the recommended Mixing Ratio

When you change the resin ratio, you should never expect to have the desired result. For example, if you add the hardener or resin more than the manufacturer's recommendations, the material will be less hard and can be robust after curing. Also, if you add too much resin more than the hardener, the material will never cure, and the surface will be sticky.

Never add Water to the Epoxy Resin

When your resin is in its liquid form, never allow it to come in contact with water or moisture. This can negatively affect its quality and the finished product. Therefore, before you mix it, thoroughly clean the container and stirrers and let them dry, too.

Use sufficiently large Containers for Mixing

Normally, chemical reactions generate heat because of exothermic reactions. The extent to which it will react depends on the quantity of materials mixed. Therefore, you should consider precautions like never exceeding the limit for mixing resin and harder (all resins and hardeners have a mixture limit, which you will mostly find in the kit).

If you're doubting the mixture quantity, you can consider dividing the ingredients into two and mixing them twice separately at a different time and with a time interval. Use a large quantity when mixing to reduce the heat it will generate. Choose a wider container instead of a long one. Low-reactive resin usually generates less heat when mixing. So, if you are mixing a large quantity, choose a low-reacting resin to minimize the heat that will be generated.

Mix at the right speed

Resin doesn't have a specific mixing speed. You can't mix it fast or do so slowly. If you mix it quickly, you will have air bubbles that cannot even rise to the surface. They will be trapped in the mixture, which will cause your work to look bubbly. If you mix too slowly, the resin will not mix properly, and a poorly mixed resin will cause problems in your work, like local drying or late drying. If you leave the mixture in a container for too long, it will shorten the working time, and it may cure during the mixing process.

Ensure you mix homogeneously

When you start mixing, the mixture will be white. As you continue mixing, the epoxy will turn cloudy, and then it will begin to turn transparent. Continue the mixture until all the turbidity disappears and it becomes clear completely. Towards the end, you will see a thin, threadlike structure. Continue mixing and ensure even the image disappears.

Pour B first, then A

Epoxy usually comes in two components: the resin and the hardener. To have a perfect blend, pour the hardener first, followed by the epoxy. This will enable the two to mix more easily and faster. And because of the density difference between the two, too much epoxy will not stick to the edges of the mixing container. Don't forget to always close the bottle after pouring. If the bottles are the same, use different color caps to close them. Ensure you use the correct cap to close each component because without doing this, the cap will easily slip through the bottle's mouth, and when you try to open it the next time, it won't open due to a chemical reaction.

TIPS FOR POURING RESIN

One aspect of resin that looks simple but needs careful consideration is the pouring part. You will often see professional resin users having bubbles in the mixture and cannot understand what went wrong despite being careful during the mixing time. The issue is mostly with the pouring. For example, a clumsy pour can lead to more formation of air bubbles. The best thing you should remember about resin is that each process has a unique method of executing it. So, you must take note. Here are a few tips on how you can pour resin.

Pour slowly and keep it close to the surface

When pouring, give it extra attention and ensure the container is close to the surface. If doing bigger projects like tables, pour the mixture several inches from the substrate. Remember, if you are making large projects, you will need a seal coat to prepare for the epoxy pouring step. The seal coat is mostly applied by hand. However, before you apply a seal coat, check and determine whether your art requires one. For small projects like jewelry, pour the mixture a few inches away from the surface to enable the resin to flow smoothly and create fewer air bubbles.

When pouring, squeeze the container to tighten the flow

Squeezing the container will allow the resin to flow in a tight stream. This is beneficial when inserting it into a small space without spreading it over the surface. Since you must never use the container again, it won't be bad even if you squeeze it and alter its shape.

Move smoothly across the surface as you pour

Although resin is generally self-leveling, it won't be bad if you make the process faster and smoother by moving the container intentionally while pouring the mixture. This will allow you to fill the space and identify gaps quicker than when you decide to do it later. If you discover you are short of the mixture, you can quickly mix another one and fill the areas before it cures.

Don't scrape out residual resin when pouring

Avoid scraping residual from the edges of the container when pouring because whatever is in that area will likely be insufficiently mixed, and it will never cure perfectly; instead, it will even affect your art. This is the reason you should always mix thoroughly and ensure you have scraped every aspect of the resin that is in the corners or edges of the container.

Pour multiple layers as needed to avoid air bubbles

As I said, epoxy resin is self-leveling, meaning when you pour it, it will spread on its own until it reaches the required destination. Pouring a single layer, especially if it requires multiple layers, will only make the surface form air bubbles. To avoid this, pour multiple layers separated by intervals. For example, if you are making a high-quality tabletop, it will self-level at ⅛ inch. So if you want to have ¼ inch coat on the tabletop epoxy, you must have multiple layers.

To apply the resin

- Start by pouring one layer normally, let the epoxy self-level, and ensure enough coat for the surface.

- Use a heating tool to remove air bubbles. You should check the instructions written in the heating tool pack on how to use it. After removing the first batch of airs, wait for a few minutes before you do it again.

- After putting one layer, wait for five to six hours for it to cure before you pour the next layer.

- Repeat this process, then add a second layer. Even though the two layers are poured at different times, they cure. Differently, it will still look perfect and seamless, and it will look as if you do a single layer without any air bubbles that will probably come with it being you do one layer.

How to Get a Smooth Epoxy Finishing

When it comes to getting a smooth finish on your art, there are two options you should consider. First, consider light sanding it, then apply the finishing product or a top coating of epoxy on the art. Either choice can give you an excellent result. So, let's look at how to achieve each of them.

Method one: Sanding the epoxy

Sanding epoxy is one of the two methods you can consider. However, you should note that when the epoxy has cured, it will be difficult to cure it because the surface has already become hard. Also, the surface hardness will make the sandpaper dull and clogged fast. Therefore, using this method, use wet sandpaper because the abrasive paper will not clog to the product.

Still, keep in mind that if you are working on a wood, using a dry sandpaper will be the best method than using a wet one. Before you sand the epoxy, let it cure completely, which normally takes around

72 hours or more, depending on your project. Sanding epoxy before curing will lead to disastrous results. So, you should wait for 72 hours. To send the art, dip the waterproof sandpaper in water or use a spray bottle filled with water and spray it on the sandpaper.

After this, sand the surface in a circular motion until you can't find any trace of the previous grain. If you wish to check your progress, use a cloth to remove the sandpaper. Once the epoxy, gently clean the surface with a paper towel. Don't use old rags because they may contaminate the surface.

If you paint the surface immediately after the sanding, you will require an electrostatic dust cloth to eliminate the remnant particles. The last step is painting the art. You can choose a different finishing product or apply another epoxy coat. Ensure you use an accurate mixing ratio to have an even surface.

Method two: Applying the Second Coat of Epoxy

The other method for getting a smooth finish is applying a second coat of epoxy. This will solve any damage made on the initial coat. You will also fix common mistakes like bubbles and uneven surfaces. But you must also be careful during this method to avoid creating another disaster. Therefore, before you apply the second epoxy coat, sand the whole surface; ensure you let it cure completely before you sand it.

For the best result, use waterproof sandpaper and drip inside warm water before using it. Next, mix the ingredients using the manufacturer's mixing ratio. Once they are well mixed, pour ⅛ of the mixture onto the surface and let it cure for about 72 hours. Depending on your project, you can apply the epoxy finishing as many layers as you want until you get a satisfactory result.

CHAPTER

6

BUILDING EPOXY CASTING MOLD AND PROPER CURING METHODS FOR EPOXY

In the previous chapter, we explore how you can finish your epoxy resin design with the right equipment. In this chapter, I will walk you through how you build an epoxy casting mold and proper curing methods for epoxy.

Let's dive into the real deal.

How to Build an Epoxy Casting Mold

Building an epoxy casting mold is the first step to creating a large resin project like river tables. To achieve this:

Start by preparing your workplace

Create a workplace where you will build and use the mold. Ensure you can reach every corner of the mold cavity. You can place a sheet of polyethylene over the workplace to have a quick and easy cleanup.

Choose your material

The next step is to choose your material. It's best to use tape to clad the base and wall components of the mold. The best materials here are melamine, medium-density fiberboard, or smooth plywood. If you are thinking about using other materials, know that it will stick to wood, glass, and aluminum. And it won't stick to sheathing tape, Teflon, polyethylene, polypropylene, high-density polyethylene, nylon, mylar, and silicone.

Design your mold

When designing your mold, ensure the wall is thick and taller than the wood slab. It's best to be ½ above the top of the pour. Extending the base surface above will let you see when areas need patching. This will also make it easy to dissemble the mold after the resin has dried.

Prevent adhesion to your mold

Use an epoxy mold release tape to cover all the mold cavity surfaces. This will prevent the epoxy from sticking to the mold and allow easy removal. Make sure you flatten the tape and seal the mold surface.

Assemble the mold

Once you cover all the surfaces of the mold in mold release tape, drip pilot holes to help with assembling the walls and base. Use screws and pilot holes to assemble the walls and base. It's best to use screws for assembling to make it easy during dissembling and when using it again. To further protect it from leaking, you can consider applying a bead of silicone on the bottom of the walls to seal the area where the wall meets the base.

Seal your mold

Your mold cavity should always be clean from dust and other contaminants before sealing the edge. To remove dust or debris, use clothes that are denatured with alcohol. Put a bead of silicone along the inner cavity of the mold to prevent the epoxy from leaking out of the mold. Ensure you spread and smoothen the bead accurately to fill the seam and let the silicone set, then pour the epoxy. As a beginner, you should consider adding a fillet of silicone to the outer edges of the wall and base to prevent leakage.

Get the project ready to pour the mixture

Level your mild on the working surface. If necessary, put the mold on wooden blocks so you can easily access the mold bottom for clamping the wood slabs. If you use shims, washers, or any other item available, you must adjust the level where necessary. Next, add the embedded item to the mold cavity. Be careful and climb the object to prevent it from floating while casting.

Mix and pour your epoxy

Now you are done with the preparation, your next step is pouring the mixture. Refer to the manufacturer's instructions for specific mixing ratio, pour depth, multi-layer pour, and cure time.

Demolding the project

Once the art has cured completely, you can use a knife to remove the mold walls. Note that the base material you added will provide leverage points for demolding.

PROPER CURING METHODS FOR RESIN

Look for a fast-curing resin to dry your work faster

Resins are manufactured by different brands, which means they cure differently. Look for an epoxy with a fast or quick cure written on the pack. Still, the slow-curing epoxy has its advantages, depending on your preference. For instance, it's stronger and water-resistant than quick-curing epoxy. It also gives you more time to work with it because it will remain soft and liquid longer than fast epoxy.

Preheat the epoxy with warm water for fast-curing

Warming the epoxy will let it settle and cure quicker than if you don't warm it. Fill a warm water bucket and let the resin sit for 10-15 minutes. The water should not be too hot, and it should be lukewarm. Also, you should heat the resin and the hardener simultaneously. The two having different temperatures will prevent them from mixing and curing properly. Always mix the resin and hardener according to the manufacturer's mixing ratio.

Avoid mixing too much die or pigment

Adding too many external components can impair the resin properties. But it's okay to add a little bit of liquid or powder pigment to give the resin color. If the pigment is more than 7%, it will stop the resin from curing appropriately.

Keep the temperature in your working space 70-80°F

Resin is sensitive to heat, and in cool conditions, it will take longer to dry and may not even cure properly. Therefore, keep your work warm and control the temperature. The ideal temperature varies between 20°C to 25°C. You should check the package for the specific temperature requirements. If you don't want your whole workspace to be hot, you can consider using heat lamps or space heaters to raise the temperature around your object instantly.

Allow the resin to cure

The time required for all resins to cure is never less than 72 hours. The specific time varies with the brand you use and the kind of product you make. Check the package for guidelines on how long the resin usually takes to cure. Avoid touching the resin before it finishes curing because it will cause the work to smudge or create bumps on the surface.

CHAPTER

7

DIY RESIN ART PROJECTS FOR BEGINNERS

As a beginner, there are many ways you can practice with resin. You can make trays, simple jewelry, coasters, wall art, and more. In this chapter, we will look at a step-by-step guide on how to make simple resin crafts specifically for beginners. So, without further ado, let's get started.

TRAYS

Resin trays are trays made from a resin mixture. The trays are unique, beautiful, affordable, and among the best gifts you will give someone. Doing this resin tray is one of the best things you can do as a beginner. So, let's look at how to make a DIY dried flower resin tray, a DIY ocean wave resin tray, and a DIY glitter resin and white tray.

DIY dried flower resin tray

Materials needed

- Epoxy Resin
- Tray Mold
- Dried Flowers and Leaves
- Stickers (You can choose any sticker according to your liking.)
- Glue Gun
- Handles
- Tweezer

How to make it

- **First, assemble and arrange your materials carefully:** When you arrange them, it will solve the problem of going to and fro to get the materials.

- Secondly, mix the hardener and the resin, and ensure you follow the instructions on the manufacturer's package.

- Once the resin is mixed well, pour the first layer and be careful so you won't split it on other things. Ensure you make the resin regular and balanced to make the tray regular and flat. After pouring it, allow it to cure for a minute, then add the flowers and leaves.

- **Start adding the flowers and the leaves:** Once the resin gets sticky, use a tweezer and insert the flowers and leaves into the resin you poured, especially since they are delicate. Also, you must be careful when putting them. Additionally, be careful not to create bubbles, pluck holes, or damage the resin you poured.

- **Use stickers as decorations:** Allow the resin to cure before you add any stickers completely. For instance, if you give the tray as a wedding gift, choose a wedding day sticker depending on the occasion. To be more creative with the tray, you can consider adding creative butterflies with leaves.
- Glue the handles: Put glue on both ends of the tray handles and put it carefully on the corner of the resin you poured. Avoid misplacing the flowers or disturbing the flat area of the resin surface. Do the same process for the other handle.
- Coat resin to the top: This is the final step, so carefully pour the resin balance on the top to have a smooth surface on the tray. The entire perfection of the tray depends on this step. So, you have to be careful here. After you complete this step, let the tray cure for 72 hours or more. Then, remove the silicone mold, and here you have your beautiful dried flower resin tray.

DIY Ocean Wave Resin Tray

Materials needed

- Epoxy Resin
- Tray Mold
- Blue and White Pigment
- Stickers and Stones
- A Hair Drier
- Heat Gun
- Handles

How to do it

- **Assemble the material:** The first step in making this version of the resin tray is to assemble your material.

- Once you have all the necessary materials, pour the resin into the tray mold. It's best to be careful so you won't split the mixture on other things. Ensure you make the resin regular and balanced to make the tray regular and flat. Pour the first layer of the resin then mix it with sand, then pour the resin layer

- Now, pour the second layer at the extreme left in a top-bottom manner. You can either use a dark or blue pigment.

- Pour the third and fourth layers into the center. If you put light blue pigment at the right, then the dark blue at the center or anyhow you want it.

- Add shape stones or any material of your choice and design. Use stones to blend perfectly with the ocean team. Put them gently on the sand layer.

- **From the ocean wave:** The next step is forming the ocean wave. Watch carefully here because it's the hardest and the easiest step to fail. It's best if you make the resin a little bit sticky. Then, use your blower to blend the white resin. Increase the resin layer and blend them with the blower until you get the unique ocean wave shape. The result of the beauty and shape will depend on how you blend the colors.

- After you finish this step, enable the resin to cure for 72 hours.

- **Add the handles:** Once the resin has completely cured, you can put the handles. Put glue on each end of the handle and then put it gently on the corner of the poured resin. Do the same process for the other handle. You can use a handle of any preferred material, shape, and color. After this step, remove the silicone mold, and your ocean wave resin tray is ready.

DIY Glitter Red and White Tray

Materials needed

- Epoxy Resin
- Tray Mold
- Red, White, and Pink Pigment
- Silver Glitter
- Plastic Cups
- Stirring Stick
- Tweezer
- Finger-cot
- Heat Gun
- Stickers/Quotes
- Handles

How to do it

- **Prepare the resin and glitter:** The first thing you should do is pour the resin and glitter inside a separate container, ensure you mix the pigmented resin perfectly, and put the quantity of the pigment based on the color you want. Make sure the quantity you put doesn't pass 7%. If you want a darker color, add more pigment to the resin. You should make the resin in separate containers. Next, arrange the materials you will use in your working space. You must apply the material at the right time and place them correctly. Don't let the resin cure completely because it will reduce the beauty and leave marks on the tray.

- Next, pour the glitter and pigmented resin. You can choose to make diagonal layers circular and round or any layer of your choice. You can also put the quantity of the glitter depending on how you want it. For example, if you choose one layer of blue, you can try to select two consecutive layers of red.
- Pour the first layer of glitter in a U-shape.
- Add a layer of red pigment, but make the shape bigger.
- Next, add a thin layer of silver color paste.
- Add a layer of white-pigmented resin.
- Add a red layer, glitter, then a white layer. Repeat the same process until you fill the entire surface of the silicone mold.
- After you finish this step, let the resin cure completely. Then, add any sticker you like and quotes to make the work more appealing and captivating.
- Next, add handles. Use a heat gun and apply glue on the handles end and ensure they are aligned, then place them on the tray's sides.
- Pour another coated resin on top to make the space smoother, so the handles can bond well.

Coasters

As a beginner in resin crafts, it's time to unleash your talent. Coasters are among the favorite DIY resin arts that are perfect for beginners. It's easy and looks cute.

Here are the materials you need:

- Wax paper or kraft paper
- Respirator
- Nitrile gloves
- Safety glasses
- Round silicone molds
- Rubbing alcohol
- Clear casting kit
- Plastic cups
- Wooden stir sticks
- Heat gun or skewer
- Tweezers
- Assorted dried flowers
- Clear rubber spacers

How to do it

- **Prepare your workplace:** In every resin art you make, the first important step is preparing your workplace. Before you start making your coaster, lay the wax paper or Kraft paper to prevent the working surface from resin that might drip during the procedure. Also, wear appropriate safety gear like goggles, aprons, respiratory masks, and gloves. Ensure your working place is also well ventilated or if possible put a fan near you and open windows.

- **Clean and prepare the silicone mold:** To make coasters, you require a set of round silicone molds. Use alcohol to wipe the molds and let them dry before you mix the resin. This will prevent dust or any particles from affecting your work.

- **Mix the resin:** The most important aspect of this work is to ensure you have a perfectly mixed resin. Since this might be your first time using resin, carefully read the instructions on the resin package.

- **Pour coaster molds:** Once you have a perfectly mixed resin, slowly pour it into the silicone molds. If it forms air bubbles, use a heat gun or toothpick to prick them. Allow the resins to sit in the silicone mold for about 15 minutes.

- **Place dried flowers:** After 15 minutes, the resin is in the right state to add a dried flower. It's best to use as many small dried flowers as you can and press them. You can use flowers plugged from your garden or purchase dried and pressed flowers from the market.

- Use tweezers to put each flower on the top of the resin until you have put the amount you want. The flower will stick to the resin, but it will remain at the top. After you finish, allow the mold to sit for four hours.

- **Add a second layer of resin:** After 4 hours, you are sure the mold has dried. Mix a second batch of resin and hardener, then pour it over the flowers until the mold you fill the mold all the way. Eliminate any air bubbles that form using a heat gun and allow the mold to cure for 2 to 3 days. After that time, remove the coaster from the mold and add clear rubber spacers to the bottom of each coaster to prevent them from sliding around on your table.

WALL ARTS

Wall art is also one of the best beginner projects you can try. It's easy, and as long as you follow the instructions properly, you will have a unique result.

Materials needed

- 32 oz. Envirotex Lite resin
- Opaque pigments, Transparent dyes, or acrylic paints
- Canvas: I found a wooden board as the canvas works best
- Stir sticks and disposable measuring cups

- Disposable craft brushes
- Latex or disposable gloves
- Paper towel
- Box or tray larger than the chosen canvas
- Micro butane torch

How to do it

- If you have plywood, you can use it as a canvas. If not, you can use a board rather than a stretched canvas. All will work, but you must support the canvas center, which can be tricky. Also, ensure the canvas or anything you want to use doesn't have dirt, debris, or dust.

- **Sealing canvas:** Mix epoxy and thinly spread it on the canvas board to seal the surface. Use a heat gun or butane touch to remove any air bubbles that formed. Wood mostly tends to create air bubbles if it's not properly sealed.

- **Prepare your workspace:** In every resin art you make, the first important step is preparing your workplace. Before making your wall art, lay the newspaper or anything bigger than the canvas board to prevent the working surface from resin that might drip during the procedure. Also, wear appropriate safety gear like goggles, aprons, respiratory masks, and gloves. Make sure your working place is also well ventilated or if possible put a fan near you and open windows.

- **Mix the resin:** The most important aspect of this work is to ensure you have a perfectly mixed resin. Since this might be your first time using resin, carefully read the instructions on the resin package.

- Once you finish mixing the resin, pour it into small containers and add any colors of your choice inside each container. You can add as much number of colors as you want.

- **Pour the resin:** You can start with any cup you want. Pour a small amount of each cup onto another cup until it fills. Then, pour the cup on the center of the canvas. You can decide to pour it on any area since you are making wall art, but you can still follow the one in this book: pouring it on the center. If the first pour isn't enough to cover the whole canvas, you can make another mixture of colors again and pour it the way you did with the first cup. After this pour, you might still need it on the edges. So, take each cup and pour it into the bare spots. You can pour some colors over the top to add more character. You can do however you want on this.

- **Pop bubbles:** The resin might have probably created bubbles. Rest assured, this isn't a big deal. Use a heat gun or microbutane to run a flame over the top of the art and pop all the bubbles. At times, you may need to wait for about 10 minutes after the pour to let the air bubbles rise to the top.

- Now, you are done with the art. Keep it aside and let it cure for at least 24 hours. Make sure you keep it in a clean place so dirt or dust won't touch it.

- After 24 hours, look back at the amazing craft you have created in your first attempt.

JEWELRY

With resin, you can make as many jewelry as you want. You can make glitter resin jewelry, pressed leaves or flower jewelry, leaf skeleton jewelry, clay jewelry with resin coating, alcohol ink design and resin, opal, wood and resin, gemstones, and many more. So, let's look at how you can create these incredible pieces.

Materials needed

- Get your resin and your hardener
- Obtain safety tools such as gloves, drop clothes, apron, respiratory mask, and goggles
- Safety gear: latex gloves, drop cloths, and apron (respirator and safety glasses are highly recommended)
- Spatula and plastic mixing spoons

- Measuring cup (it's better to use small ones since you are making jewelry)
- Jewelry bezels, molds, or casing
- Decorative items, like flowers, glitter, or shells

How to do it

- **Gather the supplies you need:** I have already listed the items you will use for this work.

- **Prepare your working space:** In every resin art you will make, the first important step after you finish gathering your supplies is preparing your workplace. Before you start making your wall art, ensure you wear appropriate safety gear like goggles, aprons, respiratory masks, and gloves. Make sure your working place is also well ventilated or if possible put a fan near you and open windows.

- **Prep Your Bezels/Molds and Decorative Items:** Before you begin the work, ensure you have the jewelry items ready. Select your bezels, molds, or casings, and keep the flowers or casting you use close by. Different casting needs different preparation to get them ready for the liquid.

- **Mix the resin:** The most important aspect of this work is to ensure you have a perfectly mixed resin. Since this might be your first time using resin, carefully read the instructions on the resin package.

- **Pour the first layer of resin:** Once your jewelry and everything is ready, pour the first layer of resin. Since jewelry is a small item, you will mix the resin in a small container to make it easy to pour and prevent it from making a mess in your workplace. Jewelry usually requires two to three layers of resin and ensures the layers are thin. The first layer usually acts as glue for sticking the decorative things before you pour the next layer.

- **Add the decorative item to the resin:** Add your decorative item to the first layer. Use a toothpick or pin to adjust its position.

- Wait for a few hours for the first layer to cure before you add the next layer of resin. You don't have to wait for it to be fully hard, but ensure it, at least, solidifies before you add the next layer.

- Once the resin is cured (the brand you use should tell you how many hours it takes), remove the jewelry from the mold.

- After you finish the resin-making process, assemble the jewelry. This includes adding hooks if it's an earring or a chain if it's a necklace. Also, put small tools for creating casting holes in the resin.

KEYCHAINS

Resin crafts are just amazing. There are endless items you can practice with it. Keychains are one of the wonderful gifts you can give your friends, family, and loved ones. If you look at a keychain, there is something elegant and attractive about it that whoever you gift will treasure for a lifetime.

Materials needed

- Epoxy resin and hardener
- Small plastic cups
- Big plastic cup
- Toothpick
- Wood skewer
- Silicone molds
- Spatulas
- Heat gun
- Blank keychains
- Face mask
- Gloves
- Gold flakes
- Glitter powder
- Mica powder
- Resin pigment
- Dried flowers
- Scissors
- Pliers
- Tweezers
- One e-strung bead (optional)
- One e-charms (optional)

How to do it

- Prepare your workplace: In every resin art you make, the first important step is preparing your workplace. Also, wear appropriate safety gear like goggles, aprons, respiratory masks, and gloves. Make sure your working place is also well ventilated or if possible put a fan near you and open windows.

- To know how your finished key chain will look, you should start by preparing the dried flower. Lay them on your working space to get the idea of placement, and you can use different flowers and decorative additions you wish to see in your work. This part will help you save time. After mixing the resin, you won't have much time to do this because you can't mix it and leave it for a long time.

- Once you are done with this part, you should mix your resin, and this is the most important aspect of this work. Therefore, ensure you have a perfectly mixed resin. Since this might be your first time using resin, carefully read the instructions on the resin package.

- After mixing it, use a torch butane or a heat gun to prick all the air bubbles that formed in your mixture. Or allow it to sit in a hot bath for three to five minutes.

- Now, pour the first three layers you will set to make the keychain. Continue moving once you pour the resin, and if you leave it, it will become sticky and hard. Pour the layer of the resin into the molds. If it forms a bubble again, use the heat gun or microbutane to level the surface.

- Get a tweezer and gently place the flower on the resin surface. The flowers don't sink in, so cover them with another resin layer. Use a toothpick to put the flower over the resin. This stage is where you can place little flecks of gold foil and leaves.

- If you have leftover resin, mix it with colored mica powder, glitter, gold foil, or any other decorative substance and stir them with a skewer. While using colored dye, you need to use a stick and swirl a pattern to mix the color uniquely and creatively.

- After finishing the above step, let the layer set for at least 6-8 hours. You should put something on top to protect it from dust or dirt.

- After the hours, you can now pour the next layer. By now, you are familiar with the drill. So, you have to mix and stir the next batch of resin. Pour the next layer on top of the flower and cover it evenly. Use a heat gun again to eliminate air bubbles that form.

- Allow the keychain to cure the mold and ensure it is under a protective layer to protect it from dirt and dust. If you feel it has bumps or a rough surface, use sandpaper to scrub and remove the irregularities.

- Technically, you should be done, but you can work on an extra step to make the work smoother and finer. Create a small doom surface on your keychain. To make this, you require another batch of resin mixture. But this time, let it harden a little bit to get tacky, then pour small on the surface and prevent it from overflowing or reaching the edges.

- Use a pin to spread the resin on the surface. You can also dome the surface while the keychain is still inside the mold. Just ensure you don't cover the hold where the jump ring enters. You must leave this for another 12 to 14 hours to let it cure. Once you finish this, insert the key chain and jump ring through the hold, and your keychain is ready to use.

PAPERWEIGHTS

Paperweights is another incredible piece you can make as a beginner. It's easy, and you can do it yourself and gift a loved one once you're done.

Below are the materials needed:

- Clear Polyester Casting Resin
- Mixing cups
- Polyester Casting Resin Molds
- Mold Release
- Items to embed
- (examples: dandelion, succulent, fossils, and wasp paper)
- Resin decor

How to do it

- **Prepare your workplace:** In every resin art you make, the first important step is preparing your workplace. Also, wear appropriate safety gear like goggles, aprons, respiratory masks, and gloves. Make sure your working place is also well ventilated or if possible put a fan near you and open windows.

- **Mix the resin:** The most important aspect of this work is to ensure you have a perfectly mixed resin. Since this might be your first time using resin, carefully read the instructions on the resin package.

- Carefully place the item in the gel while looking upside down. You will see that the fresh flower has discolored after hardening.

- Allow the resin to sit for another couple of hours. Mix another batch and pour it on top to fill the mold. Allow it to cure for one week, pop it out, and your paperweight is ready. You will notice the green color of the succulent has decreased, but it looks unique

How to make dandelion bloom embedded paperweight

- To make this, you will follow the instructions you did in the first paperweights with a full dandelion bloom. Just carefully place it in the gelled resin and allow it to sit for some time.

- Next, fill the mold with more resin to encase the rest of the dandelion. Once it holds perfectly, pour the resin at the side and allow it to fill the spaces around the wisps. The resin will not interfere with the feather as it fills around it.

How to make wasp paper paperweight

In this project, you will use wasp paper, which has a unique zebra-striped pattern. To do this:

- Fill the mold with about a half inch of resin, slip a piece of wasp paper on the top, and gently insert it with a toothpick or pin to reach halfway. Allow it to dry, and then pop it out.

How to make a fossil-embedded paperweight

- Here, you will need cool fossils called crinoids. They look like little screws and machine parts, but they are primitive animals, similar to a sea star. You will drop them in after the resin has become a gel. They will be floating inside the resin.
- Next, you should fill them up, but be careful; the tiny fossils are fragile, so they can easily break.
- After a couple of hours, pour another batch of resin mixture to cover the fossils completely.
- Allow them to harden fully. The best way you can know whether they are hard is that they won't smell like resin at all.
- Note that these things smell. So, ensure you work in a well-ventilated area.

DIY Resin Crystals

You can find crystals and gemstones in the market, but they might be expensive, and you may not even find exactly the one you want. But thanks to epoxy resin art, whenever you find a crystal you want, you can duplicate it. Now, I will explain two methods of making crystal geodes for the arts.

What you need:

- A quartz crystal cluster
- A plastic container slightly bigger than the crystal
- Mold Making Material
- Hot glue gun (optional)
- Art Resin epoxy resin
- Disposable gloves
- Stir Sticks
- Mixing cup with easy-to-read measurement lines
- Resin Tint Colorants (optional)

How to do it

- **Prepare your workplace:** In every resin art you make, the first important step is preparing your workplace. Also, wear appropriate safety gear like goggles, aprons, respiratory masks, and gloves. Make sure your working place is also well ventilated or if possible put a fan near you and open windows.

- **Mix the resin:** The most important aspect of this work is to ensure you have a perfectly mixed resin. Since this might be your first time using resin, carefully read the instructions on the resin package.

- **Prepare the crystal container:** Look for a container slightly bigger than the crystal. It should make a perfect fit, but leave about ½ space on each side to create a strong mold you can use again. Depending on the weight of the crystal, you may be required to put a clue at the bottom of the container to make the crystal stick to it.

- Once you finish this, pour the resin into one corner of the container and let it flow over and reach the crystal. Allow it to sit for three to four hours at room temperature. When it's no longer tacky to touch, it means it's ready. To remove the mold, gently pry it from the container until it releases. You must remove the crystal after you release the mold. To do this, use a utility knife and carefully cut the mold across the top of the crystal and pry it.

Making a replica

- Follow the procedure you did for mixing the resin.
- After this, pour the mixed resin into the mold and allow it to sit for 24 hours, but if you want a full hardened art, let it sit for 72 hours.
- After the hours, the resin will become hard, and you can remove the crystal casting from the mold. Repeat this process if you want to make more pieces. The mold is strong enough to withstand it.

DIY RESIN BOOKMARK

If you have friends or loved ones who love to read, then they will probably appreciate a bookmark gift. And amazingly, you can create it for them.

Materials needed

- Resin A and B
- Rectangle molds

- Mold Release and Conditioner
- Glitter
- Metallic/foil confetti
- Mixing Cups
- Stir Sticks

How to do it

- **Prepare your workplace:** In every resin art you make, the first important step is preparing your workplace. Also, wear appropriate safety gear like goggles, aprons, respiratory masks, and gloves. Make sure your working place is also well ventilated or if possible put a fan near you and open windows.

- **Mix the resin:** The most important aspect of this work is to ensure you have a perfectly mixed resin. Since this might be your first time using resin, carefully read the instructions on the resin package. But, during this project, make sure you have arranged everything, and you are ready to start from beginning to end before you mix the resin.

- Once the resin is ready, add a little bit of glitter inside.

- Use mold release to spray the mold. Pour the mixture into the mold, fill it about ¼, and ensure it's thin.

- Next, add your embellishments.

- Allow the resin to cure for 72 hours, then remove the mold.

- Create the resin bookmark by drilling a small hole at the top and tying it on a tassel.

Building Confidence through Practical Application

As you explore how you can make resin craft, you still need to focus on how you can build confidence through practical application. You shouldn't expect to make progress on your first attempt as a beginner. Perhaps it's just passion that makes you want to venture into resin art, and it can also be because you want to make money from it. So, whichever reason, you must build confidence through practical application. To achieve this, you must be intentional. So, below are some ways you can do that.

Get things done

You can only build confidence in accomplishment. When you achieve your small and big goals, you will feel better about yourself. Think of the craft you will practice every week until you achieve your goals and become perfect. If you can achieve your small goals, there are high chances you will also achieve the big ones. You will feel like you can practice the big goals and feel confident and motivated to try them.

Monitor your progress

The best way to achieve your goals is to break them into smaller goals. For instance, if you want to become perfect at making big resin crafts, you should break it down into learning the small crafts meant for beginners before you move to the bigger ones. This way, it will be easier for you to monitor your progress. Starting big at once might not be the right idea because it will pain you more if you fail. But when you start small, even if you fail, it won't hurt that much.

Do the right thing

Most confident people live by a value system, and they usually do things based on that value system, even if it's difficult and it's not in their interest. But in your case, change this mindset. You can't build confidence when doing things you are not interested in. Do things you want, even if it's hard and consumes time. In the end, you will be proud of your achievements and accomplishments.

Exercise

Exercise is beneficial to everybody regardless of what you do. It improves your health, strengthens and enhances your memory, and many more. Stay active so you can make every craft you think of.

Be fearless

Understand that failing is never your enemy. It's the fear that cripples you. When you set big goals, you will feel overwhelmed and might feel it will be difficult to do. In this moment, you should look at your inner self and muster your courage to continue going. Keep in mind that every successful person was once in your shoes. All those big people you see designing big crafts were once beginners. What they believe is that what they are going to achieve is bigger than their fear, so it's hard for them to fail. Think of how much you wish to achieve your goals and become a perfect resin artist. This will help keep your fears at bay and enable you to keep going.

CHAPTER

8

ADVANCED PROJECTS

I would love to commend your efforts for coming this far with this book. Also, I estimate that you must already mastered the art of making simple resin arts, and you are ready to try the advanced projects. In this chapter, you will learn about advanced resin projects such as flower verse, resin clocks, coffee tables, night lamps, and many more. So let's get started.

Flower verse

Seeing a flower inside your space is among the great things that can give you joy. Amazingly, you can do so with resins, and the unique part of this is that it doesn't need maintenance. It's also a great wedding gift for your friends or family.

Materials needed

- Resin kit A and b
- Shallow Glass Vase
- Artificial flowers
- Stirring Sticks
- Mixing Cups
- Latex Gloves

How to do it

- **Prepare your workplace:** In every resin art you make, the first important step is preparing your workplace. Also, wear appropriate safety gear like goggles, aprons, respiratory masks, and gloves. Make sure your working place is also well ventilated or if possible put a fan near you and open windows.

- **Mix the resin:** The most important aspect of this work is to ensure you have a perfectly mixed resin. Since this might be your first time using resin, carefully read the instructions on the resin package.

- Get a mold of any shape, depending on what you want.

- Grab your flowers and cut them according to how you want them inside the verse. Then, remove the top part and keep it aside, leaving only the stem.

- Pour the resin mixture into the mold and let it sit for about an hour.

- The one hour it will sit will make the resin gel up enough to hold the stem after you put it inside.

- Place the flower into the mold and allow it to sit for one or two days. You can choose to remove air bubbles when they form. But in this particular project, you can consider leaving them because they will look like natural water inside the vase and add appeal and coolness to it.

- After one or two days, your resin might have cured. You can now put the top part of the flower and attach it to the stem. Also, when they get dirty, you can easily remove the top and dust them, then put them back.

Trinket box

By giving this resin treasure as a gift, you will leave a lasting impact on the person you gifted. They will use the tray to decorate their jewelry and makeup items. And the fun part is that you can put the picture of the person you want to gift on the tray.

Materials needed

- Get your resin kit which includes the resin and a hardener package.
- Obtain your latex gloves, plastic cups for mixing and pouring.
- Wooden stir sticks
- Pin or toothpick
- Heat gun
- Cardboard paper
- Silicone mats
- Paper towels
- Alcohol
- Glitter, colorful mica powders, and any resin dyes/colorants
- Silicone tray molds
- Paper cut-outs, paper print-outs, dried flowers, small objects, beads, letter beads, and laminating machine
- Box or plastic bin

How to do it

- **Prepare your workplace:** In every resin art you make, the first important step is preparing your workplace. Also, wear appropriate safety gear like goggles, aprons, respiratory masks, and gloves. Make sure your working place is also well ventilated or if possible put a fan near you and open windows.

- **Mix the resin:** The most important aspect of this work is to ensure you have a perfectly mixed resin. Since this might be your first time using resin, carefully read the instructions on the resin package.

- Trace your resin mold on plane paper. If your tray mold already has a border, you can use a ruler to draw it.

- Use the template, plan your design, and see the best item to fit it, like dried flowers, paper cutouts, letter beads, or any inclusion you want. Pour the first layer and the top and pour the last at the bottom. Anything you add, if it has a right side then it must face down while you cast your layers.

- For the three layers of your tray, the first layer you will pour will be a clear resin with the photo or quotes you want to put. The second layer will be clear resin with inclusions such as dried botanicals, flowers, or glitter stars. You will then put color in the third layer.

- Prepare your precoating paper or dried flowers in resin spray or any sealant you wish to use. You can use watercolor to give your banners a slight touch of color. Then, use a laminating machine for each photo and banner to seal and protect the paper. Be careful not to cut too closely when trimming to preserve the seal. You can glue the photo and the banners together to prevent them from shifting too much inside the wet resin.

- Now, pour the first layer of resin and add inclusions.

- Cover your work with a clean box or bin to prevent dust or dirt from affecting your project. Timing the work will depend on your temperature and humidity. So, check your area or leave it overnight.

- Prepare your third layer and pour it. This is your color layer where you use colorants and mica powder.

- Cover it and let it settle so it can fully cure.

- After the curing time, you can de-mold the tray, and your tray is ready.

TUMBLER

Perhaps you have encountered many resin tumblers, and since you are now an advanced resin artist, you want to try it. So, here is a detailed way to make your resin tumbler. You can keep it for yourself or give it as a gift.

- Insulated tumbler
- Tumbler Turner Resin Obsession Crystal Doming Resin
- Resin Obsession resin opaque pigments of any color you want.
- Mixing cups
- Stir sticks

- Gloves
- Respirator mask
- Apron
- Painter's tape
- Cardboard or or plastic drop sheet
- Craft paint
- Paintbrush

How to do it

- **Prepare your workplace:** In every resin art you make, the first important step is preparing your workplace. Also, wear appropriate safety gear like goggles, aprons, respiratory masks, and gloves. Make sure your working place is also well ventilated or if possible put a fan near you and open windows.
- Paint your tumbler if it's not powder-coated. Let the paint dry between coats when you finish before adding the resin.
- When you are ready to pour the resin, ensure you cover your area completely because the resin may likely drip off the tumbler. You can use disposable scrap cardboard.
- Use a tape to cover the cup to help hold any drip, and you can feel it off later. Please take note of this point as it's important. Add tape inside the cup to catch any resin that drips.
- Mix the resin: The most important aspect of this work is to ensure you have a perfectly mixed resin. Since this might be your first time using resin, carefully read the instructions on the resin package. Once you finish mixing it, transfer it to smaller cups.

- Color the resin by adding a drop of pigment into the cups. You can add white or black to create a lighter or darker shade on the original color and mix them well.

- Start the rotation motion by turning the tumbler and adding the resin to it while letting it spin. Straighten the cup where necessary so the resin will reach it properly. Drip the resin onto the cup surface. It's best to drip each color randomly while spinning the cup. This will make you get every color on the cup. Use a stir stick to push the resin around the cup surface. Just touch the surface small, so you won't spread and over-mix it. Stick to this process until you are satisfied with the coverage. You can add resin if you want to, but it will be hard to remove.

- If you want to make the colors come together, you can use your gloved hand.

- After you finish making the spin and feel your art is okay, you can start popping the bubbles formed while the cup is still spinning. Allow it to continue spinning for four hours while the resin hardens.

- Once the resin has cured enough to stop dripping, you can turn off the turner but let the cup remain where it is for 72 hours to cure completely.

- You are almost done with the work now. Remove the tape from each end and use a dishwasher to clean the cup. You should not put tumblers made from resin into your dishwater. Instead, use your hand to wash them.

Charcuterie board

There is no better way to serve an appetizer during your next picnic than making your charcuterie board. Not only can you craft it for yourself, but charcuterie boards make an excellent gift idea that whoever you give it to will cherish for a long time. So, let's start with the items you will need to create this unique project before we move to how you can make it.

Items needed

- Epoxy Resin Kit
- Resin Obsession Opaque Pigments: White, black, blue
- Gold Leaf flakes
- Wooden Cheese Paddle
- Painter's tape
- Plastic Drop Cloth
- Heat gun

- Measuring cups
- Stir sticks
- Toothpick

How to make it

- **Prepare your workplace:** In every resin art you make, the first important step is preparing your workplace. Also, wear appropriate safety gear like goggles, aprons, respiratory masks, and gloves. Make sure your working place is also well ventilated or if possible put a fan near you and open windows. Also, look for a plastic painter's work drop sheet and spread. Use disposable cups to elevate the cheese paddle to make the resin flow easily and drip onto the protected working surface.

- Use painter's tape with a drop-down sheet to mask off the handle and some inches of the cheese paddle. Ensure you leave an adequate wooden area on the charcuterie board that won't be covered with resin because that is where you will place your fancy cheese. Cover the center of the paddle using the plastic.

- Burnish the tape onto the wood while focusing on the edge. Ensure good contact so the resin will be seeping underneath. This will give you a clean edge finishing on the board.

- **Mix the resin:** The most important aspect of this work is to ensure you have a perfectly mixed resin. Carefully read the instructions on the resin package. Once you finish mixing it, transfer it to smaller cups.

- Divide the mixed resin into three cups and add colors. The first one should have blue pigment. Add three drops of black pigment in the second cup and many drops of white inside the third cup.

- Pour the cup with white resin on the handle and spread it on the edges of the charcuterie board using the long part of the stir stick, letting it flow over.

- Next, pour the light blue and then dark blue across the surface of the board.

- By now, air bubbles might have formed. Use a heat gun to go over the surface and eliminate them. The heat gun will also blend the colors and create feathering.

- Add metal leaf onto the resin using a toothpick to create veins. Follow the pattern that the colors flow as a guide.

- Check the curing after two hours. Use a toothpick to draw a line on the resin. If it remains the same, you can move to the next step. If it flows back, you must leave it for some time to get hard. The time it takes to harden is small. Depending on the temperature of your workplace, you can check after one hour or so.

- Once you are sure the toothpick doesn't draw a line after an hour or two, remove the drop cloth from the charcuterie board. Then, carefully remove the tape from the paddle and remove the masking tape. There won't be any rough edges; instead a smooth. Let the resin cure completely for one or two nights.

- This step is optional if you want. You can apply a design to the other side. Repeat the process above to make the same design on the other side.

- Allow the resin to cure for 72 hours before using the board.

Bowl

By now, you have become a pro in using resin. So, let's take another method of making things using resin. Instead of pouring the mixture onto a mold as usual, this time, you will pour it on your working surface, and then, once it starts curing, you will shape it according to how you want it. This is the method on how you can make a resin bowl, so continue to get a headstart.

Supplies needed

- Plastic drop cloth
- Scissors
- Glass jar or plastic container
- Resin Obsession artwork resin
- Resin Obsession pigments
- Mixing cups

- Stirring sticks
- Glitters, glass beads, or metal charms
- Heat gun

How to do it

- **Prepare your workplace:** In every resin art you make, the first important step is preparing your workplace. Also, wear appropriate safety gear like goggles, aprons, respiratory masks, and gloves. Make sure your working place is also well ventilated or if possible put a fan near you and open windows.

- Obtain your plastic drop cloth. You can get this in any painter's shop nearby. Get a thick one because the thicker it is, the better the result. And peeling the resin on a thick cloth is easier than doing it on a thin one.

- Cut the plastic into a square three times larger than your working space. Select something that will serve as the bowl template to help create the form. Pull the plastic along the sides of the jar. Then, use a sharpie to draw many marks on the plastic where the plastic edges meet the jar. The marks will create boundaries of where you will pour the resin.

- Mix three ounces of resin. Look for artwork for this project because it has a short curing time, so you don't have to wait as long as the resin has partially cured. Add color to some of your resin and leave the rest aside.

- Fill the center of the plastic with color, then add some of the resin. Your marks will guide you on where you should not pour the resin.

- After you colored the center with resin, use a clear resin and circle the colored one. Don't worry, even if it gets uneven, because that will give the bowl an abstract edge.

- Use a heat gun to go over the surface and remove all the formed air bubbles.

- Add embellishments using complementary color beads of different shapes in the clear section of the resin.

- Once you feel satisfied about your art, let it cure partially. Ensure that the resin is rubbery and bendable but not completely cured. Therefore, check it every hour until it reaches this stage.

- Once the resin has softened, remove it from the clothes, squeeze it to form an abstract shape, and keep it aside to cure. To allow it to maintain its shape, keep it inside a box that will hold its sides. The jar should weigh down the center where necessary.

- After this stage, your bowl is ready. Use a dishwasher to clean the bowl. You should not put bowls made from resin into your dishwater. Instead, use your hand to wash them.

DICE

Are you going to spend some quality time at home? And I've been thinking of baking some cupcakes, but Yuk, your back is paining you. Then you considered playing some games, but unfortunately, your gaming partners aren't around. Now, what's the best thing to do than making resin dice? Wondering the best dice you should make, there are many styles options to choose from, and all fall among the seven types based on their shapes. You can identify them by the number included in the type.

Each die has a unique shape, and the numbers on the faces are different.

D4: This face has numbers from one to four. When you roll it, the number that faces up will be the one you will play.

D6: This face has numbers from one to six. The sides have dots or numerals that represent the numbers. This is the most common dice you will find.

D8: This face has numbers from one to eight. It's a double pyramid shape. It resembles a pyramid attached at its base.

D10: This face has numbers from one to ten. The odd integers on the faces meet on one side by a point, while the even integers meet on the opposite point faces. Its shape is a pentagonal trapezohedron.

D12: This face has numbers from one to twelve. Each face has a pentagon shape.

D20: This face has numbers from one to twenty. Each face is triangular, and it's the most sparkly.

D100: This face has ten sides, each with numbers from one to ten.

You can use any of these dice in dungeons or dragon games. If you want to make dice for your board game, then it's best to make D6.

Since you have picked the type of dice you want to make, it's time to choose a mold.

Supplies needed

- Mixing cups
- Resin colors
- Packing tape
- Stirring sticks
- Plastic pipettes
- Safety gloves
- Silicone mat or wax paper (to protect your table)

- Files and sandpaper to finish edges
- Acrylic paint or paint pen

How to do it

- **Prepare your workplace:** In every resin art you make, the first important step is preparing your workplace. Also, wear appropriate safety gear like goggles, aprons, respiratory masks, and gloves. Make sure your working place is also well ventilated or if possible put a fan near you and open windows.

- **Get your resin:** Often, this is where most people make mistakes. You may think it's better to get the best resin for this project, but the truth is, you should choose a resin specifically manufactured for making dice in molds. The molding part is key. Not all resin works in molds. That's why sometimes you end up with tiny microbubbles and dentable dice. Nothing goes wrong during your work, but the problem lies with the resin you use. For dice molds, it's best to use Resin Obsession Super Clear Resin. It is hard, durable, shiny, and clear. You can even de-mold it twelve hours after pouring it into the mold.

- **Prepare the mold:** The mold here has small splits on each side, which will help you de-mold. If the cuts aren't there, you won't get the resin cured. Wrap tape around the mold to make sure the resin didn't split out and to also keep the edges in place.

- **Mix the resin:** The most important aspect of this work is to ensure you have a perfectly mixed resin. Carefully read the instructions on the resin package. Once you finish mixing it, transfer it to smaller cups.

- The next step is to add colors. If you are using the Resin Obsession epoxy pigments. It doesn't take much to color the resin since the pigment is already concentrated.

- Next, pour the resin into the molds. Squeeze the sides of the mixing cup. Even if it loses shape, don't worry since you won't use it again. Gently pour the resin into the opening at the top of the mold. You can also use a pipette to pour the resin into the mold, but be gentle so air bubbles won't enter the mold.

- During the process, air bubbles might rise to the mold's opening. Keep your heat gun nearby to pop them. You should be doing this after 10-15 minutes. After you finish, allow the resin to cure for half or one day.

- After these hours, it's time to demold the resin. Remove the tape and hold the resin stem, then remove the die from the silicone mold.

- Clip your stem from the end of the die. Use sand to smoothen the edges.

- Next, highlight the numbers, use the color of acrylic paint or a paint pen, and then add it to the sides. Use a paper towel to wipe the excess.

- Now, your dice is ready. The fun part is you don't only learn how to make your dice, but you will become a game night boss.

RESIN CLOCK

Here is another unique project you can try at home with an amazing result. By now, you have greatly advanced your skills, so why not try this clock to unleash your skills? You will explore how you can make this clock, but first, let's start with the list of the supplies you need.

Supplies needed

- Wooden Clock Face
- Clock mechanism and hand kit
- Resin Spray Sealer
- Envirotex Lite Pour-On Resin
- Vinyl Gloves
- Disposable Measuring Cups (at least 4)
- Stir Sticks

- Disposable Paint Brushes
- White, Silver, and Black Acrylic Paint
- Masking Tape
- Micro-butane torch
- Wood and Resin Clock - supplies

How to do it

- **Prepare your workplace:** In every resin art you make, the first important step is preparing your workplace. Also, wear appropriate safety gear like goggles, aprons, respiratory masks, and gloves. Make sure your workplace is also well-ventilated, or if possible, put a fan near you.

- Grab your wall face and spray it with resin spray. This will seal the wood and prepare it for the resin coating. Allow the resin spray to dry fully before you move to the next step.

- Obtain your plastic drop cloth. You can get this in any painter's shop nearby. Get a thick one because the thicker it is, the better the result. And peeling the resin on a thick cloth is easier than doing it on a thin one.

- Look for a disposable cup and put it on top of the plastic drop cloth. Then, put the clock on top of it to elevate it above the working surface.

- **Mix the resin:** The most important aspect of this work is to ensure you have a perfectly mixed resin. Carefully read the instructions on the resin package. Once you finish mixing it, transfer it to smaller cups.

- You will divide the resin into three cups. The first cup will have the largest amount, and add white and a little silver paint into the cup to create a light gray color.

- In another cup with small resin, add silver.

- In the third cup with the smallest resin, add black paint.

- Stir the cups to mix them thoroughly.

- Start pouring the resin from the center, and start with the light gray onto the wooden clock face. Where necessary, use a stir stick to spread the resin. Cover the clock with the gray resin completely.

- Take the silver stick from the resin and drop it on the clock. This will make lines of the silver resin.

- Use a disposable paintbrush to break the lines to give a more realistic marbling effect. Add smaller drops of black resin.

- After having the lines, use a toothpick to write the numbers and ensure the resin didn't cover it.

- Allow the resin to sit for about 10 minutes, then use your butane torch or heat gun to pop any air bubbles.

- Let the resin cure for two hours, then come back and gently remove the masking tape around the edges. Ensure you don't touch the top of the clock face because even now, the resin is still in liquid form and sticky, and touching it will ruin it. If the tape sticks under the resin, use a micro butane torch to soften it, then peel it off.

- Allow the resin to cure for 24 hours. Then, get your kit and follow the instructions to assemble the clock. Set a time and hang your clock. You are done!

COFFEE TABLE

A resin and wood coffee table is one of the trendy items you can design. This project is for advanced users. So, you should ensure you are great at casting resin before you try this. Also, you will need a large amount of resin compared to normal small projects.

Supplies needed

- Resin
- Wood

For this project, you can use any wood of your choice, but ensure the wood is dried with moisture between 7 and 10%. If you work with wood that isn't fully dried, it will shrink and cause problems along the way. Also, choose the finishing you want. This can be a natural edge in the style of a river table or straight-sawn edges.

How to do it

- **Prepare your workplace:** In every resin art you make, the first important step is preparing your workplace. Also, wear appropriate safety gear like goggles, aprons, respiratory masks, and gloves. Make sure your workplace is also well-ventilated, or if possible, put a fan near you.

- **Measure and lay out the wooden planks:** Lay the planks close to each other in different combinations until you get the best fit. Although this stage requires some imagination, this is when you will choose how your table should look. Use a template or a ruler to find the right cut. Draw precisely at right angles where you need to saw along the wood boards using a straightedge. 2 cm in breadth and 4 cm in length are reasonable guidelines when planning this reserve.

- **Cut the plank:** Use a circular saw to cut the word to an appropriate size. Follow the marks you did in the previous step, cut the ends of the plank to level, and make them straight.

- You can use a wire brush to remove any extra bark or dirt. This step is highly important because it's where it will connect the wood. Dust or bark will interfere with your work.

- **Building your mold:** To have the best DIY resin coffee table, create a mold to hold the wood and resin in place. You can make the mold using a base plate with side ledges. You can use silk-screen plates to construct your mold. This has a waterproof coating that makes it the best for this. Rub each mold piece with a release wax, then screw them together. Use a pitcher to assemble the mold.

- **Mix the resin:** The most important aspect of this work is to ensure you have a perfectly mixed resin. Carefully read the instructions on the resin package. The resin you will need depends on the table size you will use.

- **Casting the resin and wood coffee table:** This is when you will add your resin onto the mold with resin. Put it carefully and avoid aerating it too much because this will increase the chances of forming bubbles. After you pour the resin, wait for thirty minutes so the bubbles will rise, then use a heat gun to pop the bubbles.

- It's time to shape, mill, and cut your table. After it cures, remove it from the mold, loose all screws, and then use a rubber mallet to loose the mold edges from the table. You can now mill everything to make it flat and smooth. You can also see and plane the table to the final size. Shape the table using a handheld circular saw.

- Next, sand and polish the table. Use an orbital sander and different sandpaper grit. Starts with grit 80, 100, 120, 150, 180, and 240. Remove any trace of sand between each sand before using finer sandpaper.

- After sanding the top, you can move to the other sides. Use the same sander and sandpaper grits. To have a smooth and seamless edge, ensure there is no lip between the wood and resin. After sanding the table, seal it with a thin layer of resin. Then, use grit sizes 360, 600, 1000, 2000, and 3000 to prepare the table for polishing. It's essential to work thoroughly when polishing and grinding. Do the sanding and polishing at least five times while removing sand dust after each session.

- Polish the table. This is when you will polish the table by adding the final luster. Avoid setting the rotation speed high when polishing because it will make the resin hot, and you may see unwanted spots.

- Assemble the table legs. The final step in making a resin coffee table is assembling the legs. You can consider using screw-in threaded sockets and screws to secure the legs of the tabletop. When choosing legs for your table, there is no limit. Unleash your imagination and choose any beautiful legs you want among the available varieties.

- After putting on the legs, you have a well-designed coffee table that you can use or gift to someone.

CHAPTER

9

TROUBLESHOOTING AND TIPS

You may probably experience some issues while using resin; you need not fret. In this chapter, we will cover some common issues and challenges in resin art, how to solve them, and tips for achieving your desired results.

COMMON ISSUES AND CHALLENGES IN RESIN ART AND HOW YOU CAN SOLVE THEM

Some of the issues you will encounter with resin include:

- **Resin not curing or getting hard:** This is a major problem you will encounter. In this case, many reasons might have caused this, including incorrect mixing ratios, insufficient curing time, and exposure to cool temperatures. For temperature, it's best to do your resin in a temperature range of 20° to 25°. For curing time, most reasons require 72 hours to cure completely.

- Another reason is incompatible colorant. Make sure the color you use is compatible with the resin brand you use.

- Moisture is another great problem that can alter your project. Ensure that the container used in mixing the resin or any tool you use for the work doesn't have even the slightest moisture on it.

- Resin is sticky or tacky. In this situation, the reason might be you didn't mix the resin and hardener well. It's essential to mix the materials not too slowly and not too fast. Ensure you stir and there are no steaks in the epoxy mixture. While pouring, avoid scraping the container because the resin there is probably not mixed well.

- **Bubbles:** Bubbles are inevitable when using resin. So, always have your heat gun aside. Whenever the bubbles form, you will pop them. If the bubbles are too much, maybe you don't mix the resin and hardener well.

- **Resin is cloudy:** Working at a cool temperature under 20° will make your resin cloudy. You can put the mixture inside a warm bath. You can also use a space heater in your workplace while the resin hardens.

TIPS FOR ACHIEVING THE DESIRED RESULT

When it comes to resin, the knowledge is endless. There are many ways you can achieve the desired result. Who doesn't want to stand in awe while admiring their work of art? In this part, I will share some tips for achieving the desired result with you.

- **Choose the right resin:** The first step to achieve the best result is to choose the right resin. For instance, when making dice, there is a specific resin you should purchase for this because the molding part for making dice is important. Consider the characteristics of the object you want to make before buying resin. Acrylic resin is best for making sleek, contemporary designs with an opaque finish, while bio resins, which are obtained from plants, provide an eco-friendly alternative, enabling you to create translucent and transparent projects.

- **Experiment with pigment and dyes:** Adding pigment and dyes to your work can bring life to them. Use different pigments and dyes during your work to achieve a subtle effect. Always follow the manufacturer's instructions when working with additives. Doing this will help you avoid the negative effect it could have on your resin. Ensure you check the best pigment that will work with your resin.

- **Master the mold:** A well-crafted mold is the genesis of getting the best result. You can even make your mold and use silicone molds. Also, you can experience different molds to unleash your creativity.

- **Check the mixing:** The important part of using resin is the mixing part. If you don't mix it properly, you will never get the desired results. Each resin kit comes with instructions on the mixing ratio and how you can mix the resin. Always follow the manufacturer's guidelines for this. Remember, patience is the key; rushing the work will make you end up with a result that might upset you.

- **Eliminate bubbles:** Bubbles are a common challenge when working with resin. That's why in every supply I mentioned in this book, you will either find a butane torch or heat gun, which can help you eliminate bubbles when they form. You can also use a vacuum chamber to remove the bubbles before you pour the resin into the molds.

- **Finishing touch:** After your resin cures, refine the art piece. Sometimes, you may be required to sand the edges or the entire work using sandpaper. Other times, you will use another layer of resin to cover the rough surface. You can also leave them the way they are if you are satisfied with the looks.

- Always wear protective equipment like goggles, hand gloves, and respiratory mask because it will cause skin or health problems when resin comes in contact with your body.

CHAPTER

10

EPOXY RESIN BRAND AND SUPPLIERS

Wow! We have come to the last chapter of this book. And the topic is also important and it could be a real game-changer for you. In this chapter, I will be sharing with you some of the best epoxy resin suppliers and brands you can purchase from.

Check the list below:

1. United Resin Corp, which was founded in 1970 in Royal Oak, Michigan.

2. Copps Industries, Inc., which was founded in 1979 from its base in Mequon, Wisconsin.

3. Key Resin Co., which was founded in 1993. The company has its headquarters in Batavia, OH.

4. Hapco, Inc., which was founded in 1970. The company is located in Hanover, MA.

5. CDX Industrial Adhesives & Potting Solutions, which was founded in 2000; its headquarters is in Chicago, IL.

6. Ellsworth Adhesives. The company is headquartered in Germantown, WI, and was established in 1974.

7. Specialty Polymers and Services, Inc. The company is headquartered in Valencia, CA, and was founded in 2001.

8. BJB Enterprises, Inc. was founded in 1970. They are based in Tustin, California.

9. Palmer Holland, Inc. The company has its headquarters in North Olmsted, OH, and was founded in 1925.

10. Master Bond, Inc. The company has its headquarters in Hackensack, NJ, and has been operating since its founding in 1976.

Review of Popular Epoxy Resin Brands

1. **Review on the United Resin Corp product by Irish:** "I have used several types of resin. This is my favorite so far. It cures hard, has few bubbles, and smells minimal after torching. I have had difficulty finding a resin that cures hard enough when using, especially molds that are smaller and use less resin. I have no trouble with this one. I used a resin before this one that cured hard, but the bubbles drove me crazy. I make river boards and other things. I don't have time to clean up messes caused by bubbles. I seal my wood with resin, then make the rivers by putting the resin part A in hot water for 5 minutes, mixing it with B, and pouring in layers. Success!"

2. **CDX Industrial Adhesives & Potting Solutions review from Bob Hagar:** "Very happy with the product. It looked good, had no issues, was easy to use, and had no complaints."

3. **Review from Heather:** "This product was demanding at first, and we had some sticky results in our first couple of projects because we learned after the fact that you have to stir this resin way longer than we had experienced before. But once it is stirred very thoroughly, it's amazing! It has the

longest work time I've seen with resin so far, and even after a hot water bath to jump-start the curing, we could still work with the resin longer. The tray I made took roughly 45 minutes to mix the colors/glitters and then start pouring. We still had time afterward to make a coaster with the leftovers! And because it has a long work time, it has time to let the bubbles rise for way fewer bubbles and clearer resin projects! I've bought this brand thrice and will continue to buy this one!"

WHERE TO FIND QUALITY RESIN SUPPLIERS

1. One of the leading providers of epoxy resin, Nan Ya, was established in 1958 and has operations in more than 50 different countries. Its headquarters are in Taiwan. Nan Ya has two bases in Shulin and Mailao (Taiwan) for epoxy resins and two in Kunshan (China). To meet the growing demand for epoxy resin from diverse end-user sectors, the company has gradually raised its annual capacity from 18,000 MT in 1988 to more than 461,000 MT in 2015.

2. **DowDupont**: With its headquarters in Midland, the United States, DowDupont is one of the most well-known epoxy resin suppliers and employs over 98,000 people worldwide. It is an American business that emerged from the union of Dow Chemical and DuPont.

3. Chang Chun Group is a leading supplier of epoxy resin globally and was founded in 1964. The business has headquarters in Taipei, Taiwan, and more than 2000 employees work there. Epoxy resins are produced by Chang Chun using a wide range of their exclusive technology. They provide multifunctional items with high-performance ratios.

4. Hexion: One of the largest epoxy resin suppliers worldwide, headquartered in Ohio, United States. They have about 4000 workers, dispersed throughout 90 different countries. Hexion is renowned for providing various tested, continuously high-performing products to assist end customers.

5. Olin Corporation is one of the most well-known suppliers of epoxy resin in the world, with branches in over 20 different countries and over 6,400 employees. The corporation is based in Missouri, in the US. Olin Corporation has specialized in supplying cutting-edge epoxy technology for over 60 years.

Tips for Starting a Resin Art Business

You may want to turn your skills into money. Which is a good idea. In this part, I will walk you through how you can start a resin business.

1. **Please choose what you will make:** I have demonstrated how to make advanced and beginner projects. Please choose any of them that are perfect and can sell in the market. Remember, find something you are passionate about, even among the products. People will purchase and value your products when they feel you are passionate about them. The way you will sell something you are passionate about is different from selling random products.

2. **Create your inventory:** Once you have chosen the product you are passionate about, create your inventory. It's best to have some stock ready to go, but be careful and don't make too many items when you don't have many buyers. If you

have been doing resin for a while, you probably know what's happening in the industry. If you are stuck about what to sell, then use social media to create a poll about specific items you feel are good among your creations. Remember, resin art became famous in 2020 during the pandemic. So, there has been increased completion. What will make you stand out is the quality of your work and good customer service.

3. **Get the best supplies:** The best supplies will give you the best result. Research the items that you will use and get the best deal. Please don't go for cheap items unless necessary, but you can go for those in promo and bonanzas.

4. **Check safety precautions:** Safety should be a priority in your business. Resin is an exothermic substance so that it can generate heat. Initially, your workplace should be equipped with safety tools and ensure it is well-ventilated. Make sure children or animals don't visit the place. You don't want your customers to complain that the product they bought has dust or dog hair.

5. Next, set up your shop. Online is the best, but you can still set up a physical shop. But having an online presence is crucial too.

6. Marketing! This might sound scary, but believe me, it's nothing like that. The best part of resin is that it's aesthetically beautiful, so you don't have to put much pressure on yourself to advertise. People may likely find it appealing if what you create is good.

CONCLUSION

I must commend you for your commitment so far. This book has taken you on a comprehensive journey through the captivating world of epoxy resin art. And I can tell that it has been amazing. We started by exploring the essence of epoxy resin and its historical significance in the art realm. Then, you were equipped with the essential tools and knowledge required to embark on your resin art journey, ensuring your safety and success. Also, you've learned the art of selecting the right resin and mastering basic techniques, from mixing to curing, to create stunning resin projects. From beginner to advanced levels, we've guided you through exciting DIY projects, encouraging your creativity and experimentation.

Additionally, I've provided you with troubleshooting insights and expert tips to help you overcome challenges and achieve your desired results. The book also includes valuable information on epoxy resin brands and suppliers to facilitate your resin art endeavors. Whether you're a novice or a seasoned artist, this book aims to inspire and empower you to create beautiful resin art, providing the guidance and encouragement you need to embark on an exciting and fulfilling artistic journey with epoxy resin.

Now, I estimate that you have all you need to excel as a beginner. So, ensure you put everything you've learned into practice.

I wish you luck as you go deeper into the world of epoxy resin art.

Made in the USA
Monee, IL
23 November 2024